Mary Jones

and

her Bible

Mary Ropes

CHRISTIAN FOCUS

© 2000 Christian Focus Publications
reprinted 2002; 2003; 2006
ISBN: 1-85792-568-8

Published by
Christian Focus Publications Ltd,
Geanies House, Fearn, Tain, Ross-shire
IV20 1TW, Scotland, Great Britain

www.christianfocus.com
email:info@christianfocus.com

Cover illustration by Albert Anker
Cover design by Catherine MacKenzie.
Black and white illustrations
by Stuart Mingham.

Printed and bound in Denmark
by Nørhaven Paperback A/S, Viborg.

Contents

This little book tells how one of the least of seeds grew to be the greatest of trees.

At the Foot of the Mountain

O Shepherd of all the flock of God,
Watch over thy lambs and feed them;
For Thou alone, through the rugged paths,
in the way of life canst lead them.

It would be hard to find a lovelier, more picturesque spot than the valley on the south-west side of Cader Idris mountain, where the little village of Llanfihangel-y-Pennant nestles.

Above it towers the majestic mountain with its dark crags, its rocky precipices, and its steep ascents while stretching away in the distance to the west lies the bold shore and glistening waters of Cardigan Bay where the white breakers come rolling in and dash into foam, only to gather afresh, and return undaunted to the charge.

The mountain, the outline of the bay and the wonderful picturesqueness of the valley are still much as they were hundreds of years ago. Still the eye of the traveller gazes in wonder at their wild beauty as other eyes of other travellers did in time gone by. But, while Nature's great landmarks remain, or undergo a change so gradual as to be almost imperceptible, man, the tenant of God's earth, is born, lives his brief life and passes away, leaving only too often hardly even a memory behind him.

And now, as in thought we stand upon the lower slopes of Cader Idris and look across the little village of Llanfihangel, we find ourselves wondering what kind of people have occupied those simple grey cottages for the last centuries; what were their histories, their habits, their toils and struggles, their sorrows and pleasures.

To those then who share our interest in the place and neighbourhood and in events connected with them, we would tell the simple tale which gives Llanfihangel a place among the justly celebrated and honoured spots in Wales. From its soil sprang a shoot which, growing strongly, soon spread forth great branches throughout the earth, becoming indeed a tree of life, whose leaves are for the healing of the nations.

In the year 1792, more than two hundred years ago, the night shadows had fallen around the little village of Llanfihangel. The season was late autumn and a cold wind was moaning and sighing among the trees, stripping them of their changed garments, only recently so fresh and green and whirling them round in eddies before laying them in shivering heaps along the narrow valley.

Pale and watery, the moon, encompassed by peaked masses of cloud that looked like another ghostly Cader Idris in the sky, had risen and now cast a faint light across a line of jutting crags, bringing into relief their sharp, ragged edges against the dark background of rolling cloud.

In pleasant contrast to the night with its threatening gloom, a warm light shone through the windows of one of the cottages that formed the village.

The light was caused by the blaze

of a fire of dried driftwood on the stone hearth while, in a simple wooden stand, a rushlight burned, throwing its somewhat uncertain brightness upon a loom where a weaver sat at work. A bench, two or three stools, a basic cupboard, and a kitchen table - these, with the loom, were all the furniture.

Standing in the centre of the room was a middle-aged woman, dressed in a cloak and a tall conical Welsh hat worn by many of the peasants of that day.

"I am sorry you cannot go, Jacob," she said. "You'll be missed at the meeting. But the same Lord Almighty who gives us the meetings for the good of our souls, sent you that wheezing of the chest for the trying of your body and spirit and we just need to be patient until He sees fit to take it away again."

"Yes, wife, and I'm thankful that I needn't be idle, but can still carry out my trade," replied Jacob Jones. "There are many a great deal worse off. But what are you waiting for, Molly? You'll be late for the service. It must be gone six o'clock."

"I'm waiting for that child and she's gone for the lantern," responded Mary Jones, whom her husband generally called Molly, to distinguish her from their daughter who was also Mary.

Jacob smiled. "The lantern! Yes, " said he, "you'll need it this dark night. 'Twas a good thought of yours, wife, to let Mary take it as regularly as you do for the child wouldn't be allowed to attend those meetings otherwise. And she does seem so eager about everything like that."

"Yes, she knows already pretty nearly all that you and I can teach her of the Bible, as we learnt it, doesn't she, Jacob? She's only eight now but I remember when she was only a wee child she would sit on your knee for hours on a Sunday and hear tell of Abraham, Joseph, David and Daniel.

There never was a girl like our Mary for Bible stories, or any stories for that matter; bless her! But here she is! You've been a long time getting that lantern, child, and we must hurry or we shall be late."

Little Mary raised a pair of bright dark eyes to her mother's face.

"Yes, mother," she replied, "I took so long because I ran to borrow neighbour William's lantern. The latch on ours won't hold and there's such a wind tonight that I knew the light would be blown out."

"There's a moon," said Mrs. Jones, "and I could have done without a lantern."

"Yes, but then you know, mother, I would have had to stay at home," responded Mary, "and I do so love to go."

"You needn't tell me that, child." laughed Molly. "Come along then, Mary. Good-bye Jacob."

"Good-bye, father dear! I wish you could come too!" cried Mary, running back to give Jacob a last kiss.

"Go your way, child, and mind you remember all you can so you can tell your old father when you come home."

Then the cottage door opened and Mary and her mother set out into the cold windy night.

The moon had disappeared now behind a thick dark cloud and little Mary's borrowed lantern was very much needed. Carefully she held it so that the light fell upon the way they had to take, a way which would have been difficult, if not dangerous, without its friendly aid.

"Thy Word is a lamp unto my feet, and a light unto my path," said Mrs Jones as she took her little daughter's hand in hers.

"Yes, mother, I was just thinking of that," replied the child. "I wish I knew ever so many more verses like this one."

"How glad I would be if your father and I could teach you more but it's years since we learned. We've got no Bible and our memories are not as good as they used to be," sighed the mother.

A walk of some length, and over a rough road, brought them at last to the little meeting-house where the church members belonging to the Methodist church were in the habit of attending.

They were rather late and the service

had begun but kind Farmer Evans made room for them on his bench, and found for Mrs Jones the place in the psalm-book from which the little group had been singing. Mary was the only child there but her face was so grave and her manner so solemn and reverent that no one looking at her could have felt that she was out of place. The church members who met there from time to time had come to look upon this little girl as one of their number and welcomed her accordingly.

When the meeting was over and Mary, having relighted her lantern, was ready to accompany her mother home, Farmer Evans put his great broad hand upon the child's shoulder, saying, "Well, my little maid! You're rather young for these meetings but the Lord has need of lambs as well as sheep and He is well pleased when the lambs learn to hear His voice early, even in their tender years."

Then with a gentle fatherly caress

the good, old man released the child and turned away, carrying with him the memory of that earnest intelligent face, happy in its intentness, joyful in its solemnity, having in its expression a promise of future excellence and power for good.

"Why haven't we a Bible of our own, mother?" asked Mary as she trotted homeward, lantern in hand.

"Because Bibles are scarce, child, and we're too poor to pay the price of one. A weaver's is an honest trade,

Mary but we don't get rich by it. We think ourselves happy if we can keep the wolf from the door and have clothes to cover us. Still, precious as the Word of God would be in our hands, more precious are its teachings and its truths in our hearts. I tell you, my little girl, they who have learned the love of God have learned the greatest truth that even the Bible can teach them. Those who are trusting the Saviour for their pardon and peace and for eternal life at last can wait patiently for a fuller knowledge of His word and will."

"I suppose you can wait, mother, because you've waited so long that you're used to it," replied the child; "but it's harder for me. Every time I hear something read out of the Bible I long to hear more and when I can read it will be harder still."

Mrs Jones was about to answer, when she stumbled over a stone, and fell, though fortunately without hurting herself. Mary's thoughts were so full of what she had been saying that she had become careless in the management of the lantern and her mother, not seeing the stone, had struck her foot against it.

"Ah, child! It's the present duties after all that we must look after most," said Molly, as she got slowly up; "and even a fall may teach us a lesson, Mary. The very Word of God itself, which is a lamp to our feet and a light to our path, can't save us from many a tumble if we don't use it aright and let the light shine on our daily life, helping us in its smallest duties and cares. Remember this, my little Mary."

And little Mary did remember this and her later life proved she had taken the lesson to heart - a simple lesson, taught by a simple, unlearned handmaid of the Lord but a lesson which the child treasured up in her very heart of hearts.

The One Great Need

For this I know, whate'er of earthly good
Fall to the portion of immortal man,
Still unfulfill'd in him is God's great plan,
And Heaven's richest gift misunderstood,
Until the Word of Life - exhaustless store
Of light and truth - be his for evermore.

In the homes of the poor, where the time of the elder members of the family is precious, they being the breadwinners of the household, the little ones learnt to be useful very early. Often we read of little girls of six who took entire charge of a younger brother and sister while many children of that age ran errands, did simple shopping and made themselves of very real and substantial use.

Such was the case in the family of Jacob Jones. Jacob and Molly were engaged in weaving the woollen cloth, so much of which used to be made in Wales. So, many of the household duties were left for Mary to do and at an age when children of richer parents were playing and amusing themselves with their dolls or picture-books, our little maid was busy sweeping, dusting, scrubbing, digging and weeding.

It was Mary who fed the few hens and looked for their eggs which they so often laid in strange and unusual

places, rather than in the nest. It was
Mary who took care of the hive, and

who never feared the bees. It was
Mary again who, when more active
duties were done, would draw a low
stool towards the hearth in winter or
outside the cottage door in summer
and try to make or mend her own
little simple garments whilst singing

to herself in Welsh a verse or two of the old-fashioned metrical version of the Psalms or repeating texts which she had picked up and retained in her quick, eager little brain.

In the long, light summer evenings it was her delight to sit where she could see the majestic form of Cader Idris with its changing lights and shadows, as the sun sank lower and lower in the horizon. And in her childish imagination this mountain was made to play many a part as she recalled the stories which her parents had told her and the chapters she had learned to read at chapel.

Now, Cader Idris was the mountain in the land of Moriah where Abraham was sent on his painful mission with Isaac. Mary would fix her great dark eyes upon the rocky steeps before her until she almost felt she could see the respected Abraham and his son toiling up towards the appointed place of sacrifice, the lad bearing the wood for the burnt-offering.

More and more vividly the whole scene would grow in the child's imagination until the picture seemed to be almost a reality and she could imagine that she heard the patriarch's voice carried faintly to her ear by the breeze that fanned her cheek - a voice that replied pathetically to his son's question, in the words, "My son, the Lord will provide Himself a lamb for the burnt-offering."

Then the scene would change; night was drawing near and Cader Idris, assuming softer outlines, was the mountain where the Saviour went to pray.

Leaving the thronging multitude who had been dwelling upon His every word, leaving even His disciples whom He so loved, there was Jesus - alone apart from the Eternal Father's presence - praying, and so refreshing His weary spirit after the work, trials and sorrows of the day.

"If I'd only lived in those days,"

sighed little Mary sometimes, "how I would have loved Him and He'd have taught me, perhaps, as He did those two who walked such a long way with Him on the road to Emmaus, without knowing that it was Jesus. Only I think *I* would have known Him, just through love."

Nor was it only the mountain with which Mary associated scenes from sacred history or the Gospels. The long, narrow valley, in the upper end of which Llanfihangel was situated, ran down to the sea not far away at a place called Towyn. And when the child happened to be there she would steal a few moments to sit down on the shore, gaze across the blue-green waters of Cardigan Bay and dream of the Sea of Galilee and of the Saviour who walked upon its waters - who stilled their raging with a word. Sometimes He even chose to make His pulpit out of a boat and preach like that to the congregation that stood upon the shore and clustered to the very edge of the water so that they might not lose a word of the precious things that He spoke. It will be seen, therefore, that upon Mary's mind a deep and lasting impression was made by all that she had heard and child though she might have been in years, there were real evidences of an earnest, energetic nature, an intelligent brain, and a warm, loving heart.

One afternoon, when Jacob and his wife were seated at their looms and Mary was sewing a patch into an almost worn-out garment of her own, a little tap at the door was followed by the entrance of Mrs Evans, the good farmer's wife, a kind, motherly and in some respects distinguished woman who was looked up to and loved by many of the Llanfihangel villagers.

"Good day , neighbours!" she said, cheerily, her attractive face all aglow. "Jacob, how is your chest feeling? Bad, I'm afraid, as I haven't seen you out of late. Molly, you're looking hearty as usual, and my little Mary, too - Toddles, as I used to call you when you were not much more than a baby and running round on your sturdy pins as fast as many a bigger child. Don't I remember you then! A mere baby as I said and yet you'd keep stiller than any mouse if your father there would make up a story you would understand, more particularly if it was out of the Bible. Daniel and the Lions, David and the Giant or Peter in the Prison - these were the favourites then. Yes, and the history of Joseph and his brothers; only you used to cry when the naughty brothers put Joseph in the pit and went home and told Jacob that wicked lie that almost broke the old man's heart."

"She's as fond of anything of that sort now as she was then," said Jacob Jones, pausing in his work, "or rather she's fonder than ever, ma'am. I only wish we were able to give her a bit of schooling. It seems hard for the child is willing enough and it's high time she was learning something. Why, Mrs Evans, she can't read yet and she's eight years old!"

Mary looked up, her face flushing, her eyes filled with tears.

"Oh! If I only could learn!" she cried, eagerly. "I'm such a big girl and it's so dreadful not to know how to read. If I could, I would read all the lovely stories myself and not trouble anyone to tell them."

"You forget, Mary, we've no Bible," said Molly Jones, "and we can't afford to buy one either, so dear and scarce they are."

"Yes," replied Mrs Evans, "it's a great need in our country. My husband was telling me only the other day that the scarcity of Welsh Bibles is getting to be spoken of everywhere. Even those who can afford to pay for them get them with difficulty and only by ordering them. Poor people can't get them at all. But we hope the Society for Christian Knowledge in London may print some more soon. It won't be before they're wanted."

"But with all this talk, Mrs Jones," continued the farmer's wife, "I am forgetting my errand in coming here and that was to ask if you'd any newly laid eggs. I've had a large order sent to me and our hens are laying badly, so that I can't make up the number. I've been collecting a few here and there, but I haven't enough yet."

"Mary knows more about the hens and eggs than I do," said Molly, looking at her little daughter who had not put a stitch into her patch while the talk about Bibles had been going on and whose cheeks and eyes showed in their deepened colour and light how much interest she had in what had been said.

But now the child got up half guiltily from her low seat, saying, "I'll get what we have to show you, Mrs Evans."

Soon she came in with a little basket

containing about a dozen eggs. The farmer's wife put them into her bag, then patting Mary's pink cheeks, rose to take her leave, after paying for the eggs.

"And remember this, little maid," she said, kindly, when, after saying good-bye to Jacob and Molly, she

was taking leave of Mary at the door. "Remember this, my dear little girl. As soon as you know how to read (if by that time you still have no Bible) you shall come to the farm when you like and read and study ours - that is, if you can manage to get so far."

"It's only two miles, that's nothing!" said sturdy Mary with a glance down at her strong little bare feet. "I'd walk further than that for such a pleasure, ma'am" Then she added with a less joyful ring in her voice, "At least, I would, if ever I *did* learn to read!"

"Never mind, little woman! The likes of you wasn't made to sit in the dark always, " replied Mrs Evans in her cheery, comforting tones. "The Lord made the want and He'll satisfy it; be very sure of that. Remember, Mary, when the multitude that waited on the Saviour were hungry the Lord did not send them away empty though no one saw how they were to be fed. He'll take care you get the bread of life too, although it seems so unlikely now. Good-bye and God bless you, my child!" and good Mrs Evans, with a parting nod to the weaver and his wife and another to Mary, went out and got into her little pony-cart, which was waiting for her in the road, under the care of one of the farm-boys.

Mary stood at the door and watched

their visitor till she was out of sight. Then, before she closed the door, she clasped her small brown hands against her chest and her thoughts formed themselves into a prayer something like this, "Dear Lord who gave bread to the hungry folk in Bible times, and did teach and bless even the poorest, please let me learn and not grow up in darkness."

Then she shut the door and came and sat down, resolving in her childish heart that if God heard and answered her prayer and she learned to read His Word she would do what she could, all her life long, to help others as she herself had been helped.

Coming to the Light

O thou who out of the darkness
Reachest thy trembling hand,
Whose ears are open to welcome
Glad news of a better land;
Not always shalt thou be groping,
Night's shadows are well-nigh past:
The heart that for light is yearning
Attains to that light at last.

Two years had passed away since Mrs Evans's visit, as recorded in the preceding chapter, and still little Mary's prayer seemed as far as ever from being answered.

With the industry and patience of more mature years the child went about her daily duties and her mother depended upon her for many things which do not generally form part of a child's occupations. Mary had less time for dreaming now and though Cader Idris was still the spot with which her imagination associated Bible scenes and pictures, she had little time for anything but her everyday duties.

She still accompanied her mother to the meetings and so, from continually coming into contact with older people rather than children of her own age, Mary had grown more grave and earnest in face and manner and would have been called old-fashioned if she had lived in a place where any difference was known between old fashions and new.

It was about this time that Jacob Jones came home one evening from Abergynolwyn - a village two miles away from Llanfihangel - where he had been selling the woollen cloth which he and Molly had been making during the past months.

Jacob had been away for most of the day yet he did not seem tired. His eyes were bright and his lips wore a smile as he entered the cottage and sat down in his usual place in the corner, by the chimney .

Mary, whose observant eye rarely failed to note the least change in her father's face and manner, ran towards him and stood before him, looking at his bright face searchingly.

"What is it, father?" she said, her own dark eyes flashing back the light in his. "Something good has happened, or you wouldn't look like that!"

"What a sharp-eyed little girl this is!" replied Jacob, fondly, drawing the child nearer and seating her upon his knee. "What a very sharp-eyed little woman to find out that her old father has something to tell!"

"And is it something that concerns me, father?" asked Mary, gently stroking Jacob's face.

"It *is* something that concerns you most of all, my chick, and us through you."

"What can it be?" murmured Mary, with a quick, impatient little sigh.

"What is it, father?" asked Mrs. Jones, "we both want to know."

"Well," replied Jacob, "what would you say, Molly dear, to our little daughter here becoming a learned woman, knowing how to read, write and count and all a great deal better than her parents ever did before her?"

"Oh, father!"

The exclamation came from Mary who in her excitement had slipped from Jacob's knee and now stood facing him, breathless with suspense, her hands closely clasped.

Jacob looked at her a moment without speaking; then he said tenderly, "Yes, child, there *is* a school to be opened at Abergynolwyn. A schoolmaster is chosen already and as my little Mary thinks nothing of a two miles' walk she shall go and learn all she can."

"Oh, father!"

"Well," continued Jacob, now laughing outright, "how many 'Oh fathers!' are we going to have? But I thought you'd be glad, my girl, and I was not wrong. You are pleased, dear, aren't you?"

There was a pause; then Mary's reply came, low spoken, but with such deep contentment in its tones.

"Pleased, father? Yes, indeed, for now I shall learn to read the Bible."

Then a thought struck her and a shadow came across the happy face as she said, "But mother, perhaps you won't be able to spare me?"

"Spare you? Yes, I will, child,

though I can't deny that it will be difficult for me to do without my little right hand and help. But for your good, my girl, I would do harder things than that."

"Dear, good mother!" cried Mary, putting an arm about Molly's neck and kissing her. "But I don't want you to work too hard and tire yourself. I'll get up earlier and do all I can before school." Then as the child sat down again to her work, her heart, in its joyfulness, sent up a song of thanksgiving to the Lord who had heard her prayer and opened the way for her to learn, that she might not grow up in darkness.

After a while, Jacob went on.

"I went to see the room where the school is to be held and who should come in while I was there but Mr. Charles of Bala. I'd often heard of him before but I'd never seen him and I was glad to set eyes on him for once."

"What did he look like, Jacob?" asked Molly.

"Well, Molly, I never was a very good one for drawing a portrait but I should say he was between forty and fifty years old, with a fine big forehead. His face isn't anything so *very* special until he smiles but when he does it's like sunshine which goes to your heart and warms you right through. Now I've seen him and heard him speak I can understand how he does so much good. I hear he's going about from place to place opening schools for the poor children who would grow up ignorant otherwise."

"Like me," murmured Mary, under her breath.

"And who's the master that's to be set over the school at Abergynolwyn?" asked Molly.

"I heard that his name is John Ellis," replied Jacob, "a good man and right for the work, so they say and I hope it'll prove so."

"And how soon is the school to open, Jacob?" asked his wife.

"In about three weeks, I believe," answered Jacob. "And now, Mary my girl if you can bring yourself to think of such a thing as supper, after everything I've been telling you, why don't you get some ready for I haven't eaten since noon."

The following three weeks passed more slowly for little Mary Jones than any three months she could remember before. Such childishness as there was in her seemed to show itself in impatience and we must confess that her home duties at this time were not so cheerfully or so punctually performed as usual, owing to the fact that her thoughts were far away, her heart being set on the thing she had longed for so earnestly.

"If *this* is the way it's going to be Jacob," said Molly to her husband one evening, "I shall wish there had never been a thought of school at Abergynolwyn. The child's head is so full of school that she goes about like

42

one in a dream; what it'll be like when that school begins, I daren't think."

"Don't you fret, wife," replied Jacob smiling. "It'll come right. Don't you see that her poor little busy brain has been longing to grow and now that there's a chance of its being fed she's all agog. But you'll find, once she gets started, she'll get on all right with her home work as well. She's but ten years old, Molly, after all, and for my own part I'm not sorry to see there's a bit of the child left in her even if it shows itself this way. She's always been such a little old woman! "

But these longest three weeks that Mary ever spent came to an end at last and Mary began to go to school, thus commencing a new era in her life.

Really hungering and thirsting after knowledge, the child found her lessons a delight. What other children called drudgery was to her only pleasure. In fact her eagerness was so great that she was almost always at the top of her class and in an incredibly short space of time she began to read and write.

The master, who had a quick eye for observing the character and talents of his pupils, soon noticed Mary's qualities and encouraged her in her pursuit of such knowledge as was taught in the school. The little girl repaid her schoolmaster's kindness by the most unwearied diligence and attention.

While the brain was being fed her heart did not grow cold nor did her practical skills fall away. Molly Jones had now no fault to find with Mary's performance of her home duties. The child rose early and did her work before breakfast and after her return from school in the afternoon she again helped her mother, only reserving for herself time enough to prepare her lessons for the next day.

At school she was a general favourite and never seemed to be regarded with jealousy by her companions, this being probably due to her friendly manner and the kind way in which she was willing to help others whenever she could.

One morning a little girl was seen to be crying sadly when she reached the school-house. On being questioned as to what was the matter, she said that on the way there a big dog had snatched at the little paper bag in which she was bringing her dinner to eat during the recess and had carried it off so she would have to go hungry all day.

Some of the pupils laughed at the child for her carelessness and some called her a coward for not running after the dog and getting back her dinner, but Mary crept up to the little one's side, whispered something in her ear, dried the wet eyes, kissed the flushed cheeks and soon the child was smiling and happy again.

But when dinner-time came Mary and the little dinnerless girl sat close together in a corner and more than half of Mary's provisions found their way to the smaller child's mouth.

The other pupils looked on, feeling somewhat ashamed that no one but Mary Jones had thought of doing so

kind and neighbourly an action at the cost of a little self-denial. But the lesson was not lost upon them and from that day Mary's influence made itself felt in the school for good.

In her studies she progressed steadily and this again gave opportunity for the development of the helpful qualities by which, from her earliest childhood, she had been well known.

On one occasion, for instance, she was just getting ready to set off on her two miles' journey home when she spied in a corner of the now deserted schoolroom a little boy with a book open before him and a smeared slate and blunt pencil by its side. The poor little fellow's tears were falling over his unfinished task and evidently he was in the last stage of childish hopelessness. He had dawdled away his time during the school hours or had not listened when the lesson had been explained. Now school discipline required that he should stay behind when the rest had gone and attend to the work which he had neglected.

Mary had a headache that day and was longing to get home, but the sight of that tearful, sad little face in the corner banished all thought of self and, as the voices of the other children died away in the distance, she crossed the room and leaned over the small student's shoulder.

"What is it, Robbie dear?" said she in her old-fashioned way and tender low-toned voice. "Oh, I see, you've got to do that sum! I can't do it for you, you know, because that would be a sort of cheating but I can tell you how to do it yourself and I think I can make it clear."

Then Mary fetched her little bit of wet rag to wash the slate and got an old knife and sharpened the pencil.

"Now," said she, smiling cheerily, "see, I'll put down the sum as it is in the book," and she wrote on the slate in clear, if not very elegant figures, the sum in question.

Encouraged, Robbie gave his mind to his task and with a little help it was soon done. Mary's light heart made up for her sore head so she trotted home, very glad that what she was herself learning could be a benefit to others.

Not long after the commencement of the day school a Sunday school also was opened and the very first Sunday that children were taught there our little friend was there, as clean and fresh as soap and water could make her, with bright eyes and eager face, showing the keen interest she felt and her great desire to learn.

That evening after the service in the little meeting-house, as the farmer's wife, good Mrs Evans, was just going to get into her pony-cart to drive home she felt a light touch on her arm while a sweet voice she knew said, "Please, ma'am, might I speak to you for a moment?"

"Surely, my child," replied the good woman, turning her beaming face on little Mary, "what have you got to say to me?"

"Two years ago, please, ma'am, you were so kind as to promise that when I'd learned to read I could come to the farm and read your Bible."

"I did, I remember it well," answered Mrs Evans. "Well, child, do you know how to read?"

"Yes, ma'am, " responded Mary; "and now I've joined the Sunday school and shall have Bible lessons to prepare

and if you'd be so kind as to let me come up to the farm one day in the week - perhaps Saturday, when I've a half-day's holiday - I could never thank you enough."

"There's no need for thanks, little woman, come and welcome! I shall expect you next Saturday and may the Lord make his Word a great blessing to you!"

Mrs Evans held Mary's hand for a moment then she got into her cart and the pony started off quickly towards home, as though he knew that old Farmer Evans was laid up with rheumatism and that his wife wished to get back to him as soon as possible.

Two Miles to a Bible

'Tis written, man shall not live alone
By the perishing bread of earth;
Thou givest the soul a richer food
To nourish the heavenly birth.
And yet to our fields of golden grain
Thou bringest the harvest morn;
Thine op'ning hand is the life of all,
For Thou preparest them corn.

Mrs Evans's farm was a curious old-fashioned place. The house was a large, rambling building with many strange ups and downs and with oddly shaped windows in all sorts of unexpected places. And yet there was an aspect of homely comfort about the house not always to be found in far finer and more imposing-looking residences. At the back were the out-buildings - the sheds and cow-houses, the poultry-pens, the stables and pig-sties. While stretching away beyond these again were the home paddock, the drying-ground and a small enclosed field which went by the name of Hospital Meadow, on account of its being used for injured animals that needed a rest.

With the farmer himself we made acquaintance two years ago at the meeting when he spoke so kindly to Mary. He was still the same good, honest, hard-working, God-fearing man, never forgetting in the claims and anxieties of his work what he owed to the Giver of all who sends His rain for the watering of the seeds and His sun for the ripening of the harvest.

Nor did he - as too many farmers were in the habit of doing - grumble at God's providences and find fault with God's dealings if the rain came down upon the hay before it was safely carried, or if an early autumn gale flattened his wheat against the earth from which it sprang before the sickle could be put into it. Nor did he complain and grumble even when disease showed itself among the breed of small but active cattle of which he was justly proud and infected some of his fine sheep, destined for the famous Welsh mutton which sometimes was to be found on English tables.

In short, he was contented with what the Lord sent and said with Job, when a misfortune occurred, "Shall we receive good at the hands of the Lord, and shall we not receive evil?"

Of Mrs Evans we have already spoken and if we add here that she was a real help to her husband, in matters both temporal and spiritual, that is all we need to say in her praise.

This worthy couple had three children. The eldest was already grown-up; she was a fine girl and a great comfort and help to her mother. The younger children were boys who went to a grammar school in a town a mile or two away: they were manly, high-spirited little fellows, well-trained and as honest and true as their parents.

Such then was the family into which Mary was welcomed with all love and kindness. She was shy and timid the first time for the farm-house was a much finer place than any home she had seen before. There was an atmosphere of warmth and delicious signs of plenty, which were unknown in Jacob Jones's poor little cottage where everything was most frugal.

But Mary's shyness did not last long; indeed it disappeared soon after she had crossed the threshold where she was met by Mrs Evans with a hearty welcome and a motherly kiss.

"Come in, little one," said the good woman, drawing her into the cosy, old-fashioned kitchen where a kettle was singing on the hob and an enticing fragrance of currant shortcake, baking for an early tea, scented the air.

"There, get warm, dear," said Mrs Evans, "and then you shall go to the parlour and study the Bible. And have you got a pencil and scrap of paper to take notes if you want them?"

"Yes, thank you, ma'am, I brought them with me," replied Mary.

For a few minutes she sat there, basking in the pleasant, cheery glow of the fire-light; then she was admitted to the parlour where, on the table in the centre of the room and covered reverently with a clean, white cloth, was the precious book.

It must not be thought from the care that was taken of it that the Bible was never used. On the contrary, it was always read at prayers night and morning and the farmer, whenever he had a spare half-hour, liked nothing better than to study the sacred book and seek to understand its teachings.

"There's no need to tell you to be careful of our Bible and to turn over the leaves gently, Mary, I'm sure," said Mrs Evans, "you would do that anyway I know. And now, my child, I'll leave you and the Bible together. When you've learned your lesson for Sunday school and read all you want come back into the kitchen and have some tea before you go."

Then the good farmer's wife went away, leaving Mary alone with a Bible for the first time in her life.

The child raised the napkin at once and, folding it neatly, laid it to one side. Then, with trembling hands, she opened the book at the fifth chapter of

John and her eyes caught these words, "Search the scriptures; for in them ye think ye have eternal life: and they are they which testify of Me."

"I will! I will!" she cried, feeling as if the words were spoken directly to her by some Divine voice. "I will search and learn all I can. Oh, if had but a Bible of my own!" And this wish, this sigh for the rare and coveted treasure, was the key-note to a grand chorus of glorious harmony which, years after, spread until it rolled in waves of sound over the whole earth. Yes, that yearning in a poor child's heart was destined to be a means of light and knowledge to millions of souls in the future. In this way, God has often chosen the weak things of the world to carry out His great designs and work His will. And here, once more, is an instance of the small beginnings which have great results - the importance of which cannot be calculated on this side of eternity.

When Mary had finished studying the Scripture lesson for the next day, and had enjoyed a plentiful meal in the cosy kitchen, she said good-bye to her kind friends and set off on her homeward journey, her mind full of the one great longing out of which a resolution was slowly shaping itself.

It was formed at last.

"I *must* have a Bible of my own!"

she said aloud, in the earnestness of her purpose. "I must have one if I save for it for ten years!" and by the time this was settled in her mind the child had reached her home.

Christmas had come and with it some holidays for Mary and the other pupils who attended the school at Abergynolwyn. Our little heroine would only have been sorry for the end of the lessons had it not been that during the holidays she had determined to commence carrying out her plan of earning something towards the purchase of a Bible.

Without neglecting her home duties, she managed to undertake little jobs of work for which the neighbours were glad to give her a little something. Sometimes it was to mind a baby while the mother was at the wash-tub. Maybe, to pick up sticks and brushwood in the woods for fuel or to help mend and patch the poor garments of the family for a worn, weary mother who was thankful to give a small sum for this timely welcome help.

And every halfpenny, every farthing was put into a rough little money-box which Jacob made for the purpose, with a hole in the lid. The box was kept in a cupboard, on a shelf where Mary could reach it and it was a real and heartfelt joy to her when she could bring her day's earnings - some little copper coins, perhaps - and drop them in, longing for the time to come when they would have swelled to the amount needed - a large sum unfortunately - for buying a Bible.

It was about this time that good Mrs Evans, knowing the child's earnest wish, made her a present of a fine cockerel and two hens.

"No, no, my dear, don't thank me," said she, when Mary was trying to tell her how grateful she was, "I've done it, first to help you along with that Bible you've set your heart on and then, too, because I love you and like to give you pleasure. So now, my child, when the hens begin to lay, which will be early in the spring, you can sell your eggs, for these will be your very own to do what you like with, and you can put the money to any use you please. I think I know what you'll do with it," added Mrs Evans with a smile.

But the first piece of silver that Mary had the satisfaction of dropping into her box was earned before she had any eggs to sell and in quite a different way from the sums which she had received up until then. She was walking one evening along the road from Towyn, where she had been sent on an errand for her father, when her foot struck against some object lying in the road. Stooping to pick it up, she found it was a large leather purse. Wondering whose it could be, the child went on until, while still within half a mile from home, she met a man walking slowly and evidently searching for something. He looked up as Mary approached, and she recognized him as Farmer Greaves, a brother-in-law of Mrs Evans.

"Ah! Good evening, Mary Jones," said he, "I've had such a loss! Coming home from market I dropped my purse, and - "

"I've just found a purse, sir," said Mary, "is this it?"

"You've found a purse?" exclaimed the farmer eagerly. "Yes indeed, my dear, that is mine and I'm very much obliged to you. No, stay a moment," he

called after her, for Mary was already trudging off again. "I should like to give you something for your honesty - I mean just a small token by way of thanks."

As he spoke, his finger and thumb closed on a bright shilling, which surely would not have been too much to give to a poor child who had found a heavy purse. But he thought better (or worse) of it and took out instead a sixpence and handed it to Mary, who took it with very heartfelt thanks and ran home as quickly as possible to drop her silver treasure safely into the box where it was destined to keep its poorer brethren company for many a long year.

But the Christmas holidays were soon over and then it was difficult for Mary to keep up with her daily lessons and her Sunday-school tasks, the latter involving the weekly visits to the farm-house for the study of the Bible. What with these and her home duties, sometimes weeks passed without her having time to earn a penny towards the purchase of the sacred treasure.

Sometimes, too, she was rather late in reaching home on the Saturday evenings and now and again Molly was uneasy about her. For Mary would come by short cuts over the hills along ways which, however safe in the daytime, were rough and unpleasant, if not dangerous, after dark and in those long winter evenings the daylight vanished very early.

It was on one of these occasions that Molly and Jacob Jones were sitting and waiting for their daughter. The old clock had already struck eight. She had never been so late as this before.

"Our Mary ought to be home, Jacob," said Molly, breaking a silence disturbed only by the noise of Jacob's busy loom. "It's got as dark as dark and there's no moon tonight. The way's a rugged one if she comes the short cut across the hill and she's not one to choose a long road if she can find a shorter one, bless her! She's more than after her time. I hope no harm's come to the child." Molly walked to the window and looked out.

"Don't be fretting yourself, Molly," replied Jacob, pausing in his work; "Mary's out on a good errand and He who put the love of good things in her heart will take care of her in her going out and in her coming in, from henceforth, even for evermore."

Jacob spoke solemnly but with a tone of conviction that comforted his wife, as words of his had often done before. Just then a light step bounded up to the door, the latch was lifted and Mary's lithe young figure entered the cottage, her dark eyes shining with intelligence, her cheeks flushed with exercise, a look of eager animation overspreading the whole of her bright face and seeming to diffuse a radiance round the cottage, which was reflected in the faces of Jacob and Molly.

"Well, child, what you have learned today?" questioned Jacob. "Have you studied your lesson for the Sunday school?"

"Ay, father, that I have and a beautiful lesson it was," responded the child. "It was the lesson and Mr. Evans together that kept me so late."

"How is that, Mary?" asked Molly. "We've been very uneasy about you, worried in case something had happened to you."

"You needn't have been so, mother dear," replied the girl, with something of her father's quiet assurance. "God knew what I was about and He would not let any harm come to me. Oh, father, the more I read about Him the more I want to know and I will not rest until I've a Bible of my own. But today I've brought home a big bit of the farmer's Bible with me."

"What do you mean, Mary? How could you do such a thing?" questioned Molly in amazement.

"Only in my head, mother dear, of course," replied the child; then in a lower voice she added, *"and my heart."*

"And what is the bit?" asked Jacob.

"It's the seventh chapter of Matthew," said Mary. "Our Sunday lesson was from the first verse to the end of the twelfth verse. But it was so easy and so beautiful that I went on and on till I'd learned the whole chapter. Just as I finished Mr Evans came in and asked me if I understood it all and when I said there were some bits that puzzled me he was so kind and explained them. If you like, mother and father, I'll repeat the chapter to you."

So Jacob pushed away his work and took his old seat in the chimney corner and Molly began some knitting, while Mary sat down on a stool at her father's feet. Then, beginning at the first verse, she repeated the whole chapter without a single mistake, without a moment's hesitation and with a tone and emphasis which showed her understanding of the truths so beautifully taught and her sympathy with them.

"Mark my words, wife," said Jacob that night, when Mary had gone to bed, "that child will do a work for the Lord before she dies. Don't you see how He Himself is leading and guiding His lamb into green pastures and beside still waters? Why, Molly, when she repeated that verse, 'Ask, and ye shall receive,' I saw her eyes shine and her cheeks glow again, and I knew she was thinking of the Bible that she's set her heart on and which I don't doubt she's praying for often enough when we know nothing about it. And the Lord, He will give it to her some day. Of that I'm certain. Yes, Molly, our Mary will have her Bible!"

Faithful in that which is Least

Since this one talent Thou hast granted me,
I give Thee thanks, and joy, in blessing Thee,
That I am worthy any
I would not hide or bury it, but rather
Use it for Thee and Thine, O Lord and
Father, And make one talent many.

We may be sure that there were many influences which moulded the character of Mary Jones during the years of her school-life, confirming in her the wonderful steadfastness of purpose and earnestness of spirit for which she was remarkable, as well as fostering the tender and loving nature that made her loved by all with whom she came in contact.

Her master, John Ellis (who afterwards was stationed at Barmouth), seems to have been a conscientious and able teacher and we can be sure that he took no small part in the development of the mind and heart of a pupil who must always have been an object of special interest from her great intelligence and eagerness to learn.

But as the years passed the time came for John Ellis to change his sphere of labour. He did so and his place was taken by a man, a summary of whose story would be relevant to share here, as he was the teacher under whom

Mary Jones was being instructed at the time when a great event occurred in her history, which you will read about in the next chapter.

The successor to John Ellis was Lewis Williams, a man , who from a low position in life and from absolute ignorance rose to a position of considerable influence and popularity; from an utterly inattentive and godless life, to be a God-fearing and noble-minded Christian.

He was a small man and from did not possess great intellect or talents. But what he lacked in mental gifts he made up for in determination and perseverance . He was born in Pennal in the year 1774 His parents were poor, but that is all we know of them.

Like many other boys in the neighbourhood, at that time, Lewis Williams was wild and reckless, breaking the Sabbath continually and being condemned by those who knew him because of how he behaved.

But when he was about eighteen years old he happened, on one occasion, to be at a prayer-meeting, when a Mr Jones of Mathafarn was reading and preaching on the fifth chapter of the Epistle to the Romans.

The word of God, told to Lewis Williams in perhaps a fresh and striking manner, was used to carry home to his hard heart the conviction of sin and from then on a change was observed in him, which gradually deepened until no-one could doubt that he had become an earnest and consistent Christian.

At the time when he went to become a member of the Methodist church at Cwmllinian, he was asked, "If Jesus Christ asked you to do some work for Him, would you do it?" His answer gives us the key to his success: "Oh yes, *whatever* Jesus required of me I would do *at once.*"

This was the start of the religious life of this unique man.

Some years later, when in service

at a place called Trychiad, near Llanegryn, he could not help but notice the ignorance of the boys in the neighbourhood and burning with enthusiasm to perform some direct and special work for his Heavenly Master he resolved to establish a Sunday school there and, if possible, a week-night school as well, in order to teach the lads to read.

This would have been an admirable thing to do but not particularly remarkable if Lewis Williams had received any sort of education himself. But as he had never enjoyed a day's schooling in his life and could hardly read a word correctly, the thought of teaching others seemed, to say the least, rather a wild idea.

But how often the old proverb has been proved true, that where there is a will there is a way and once more this was confirmed in the experience of Lewis Williams.

Because of the young man's untiring

energy and courage his school was opened in a short time and he began the work of instruction, teaching the alphabet to the lowest class by setting it to the tune of "The March of the Men of Harlech."

But Lewis Williams, if he was to be a schoolmaster at all, could hardly confine his instructions to the lowest class in the school. In teaching the older boys he was coming face to face with an obstacle which might well have seemed insurmountable to anyone who was less courageous.

Lewis Williams could not read, or at least he could not read fluently or correctly, yet he had agreed to teach reading to the lads in his school.

Being aware of how little he knew himself, before the start of his Sunday-school or evening classes, Williams used to pay a visit to a good woman called Betty Evans who had learned to read well. Under her tuition he prepared the lessons he was going to give that day or the next, so that in reality the teacher at that flourishing little school was only ahead of his pupils by a few hours.

At other times he would invite a number of students from a high school in the neighbourhood to come for reading and discussion.

With quiet tact and careful planning, he would arrange that the subject taken for reading and discussion would include the lesson which he would shortly have to give.

While the reading and talk went on Williams listened with close attention. The discussions on the meaning or pronunciation of the more difficult words was all of benefit to him as they familiarised his mind with what he needed to know.

But none of the young people who met like this had any idea that the man who invited them, who spoke so discreetly and listened so attentively, was himself a learner and dependent on them for the proper construction of phrases or for the correct pronunciation of words that would come up in his next day's or week's lessons.

The school duties always began with prayer and as the teacher had a restless, unruly set of lads to deal with he invented a somewhat unique way of getting their attention for the devotions which he led them in.

Familiar with military exercises through former experiences in the army, he would put the restless boys through a series of these and when they came to "stand at ease," and "attention!" he would at once, but very briefly and simply, engage in prayer.

While Lewis Williams was hard at work at Llanegryn, seeking to win hearts for the Saviour and train minds to serve Him, it so happened that Mr Charles of Bala, who was to lead a members' meeting to be held at Abergynolwyn, arrived at Bryncrug the evening before and spent the night at the house of John Jones, the schoolmaster of that place.

In the course of conversation with his host, Mr Charles asked him if he knew of a suitable person to undertake the charge of one of his recently established schools in the neighbourhood. John Jones replied that he had heard of a young man at Llanegryn who taught the children both on week-nights and Sundays; "but" added the schoolmaster, "as I hear that he himself cannot read I can hardly understand how he is able to instruct others."

"Impossible!" exclaimed Mr Charles. "How can anyone teach what he does not himself know?"

"Still, they say he does," replied John Jones.

Mr Charles at once expressed a wish to see this mysterious teacher of youth, who was reported as passing on to others what he did not himself know. The next day, having been asked by

John Jones, our young schoolmaster made his appearance. His rustic dress and the simplicity of his manner gave the impression of his being anything but a teacher, whatever might have been said of him.

"Well, my young friend," said Mr Charles, in the warm and pleasant way that was natural to him and that at once inspired with confidence all who dealt with him, "they tell me you keep a school at Llanegryn on Sundays and week-nights, for the purpose of teaching children to read. Have you many students?"

"Yes, sir, far more than I am able to teach," replied Lewis Williams.

"And do they learn a little by your teaching?" asked Mr Charles, as kindly as ever but with a quaint smile lurking round his mouth.

"I think some of them learn, sir," responded the young teacher, very modestly and with an overwhelming sense of his own ignorance - a consciousness that showed itself painfully both in his voice and manner.

"Do you understand any English?" questioned Mr Charles.

"Only a word or two, sir, which I picked up when serving in the army."

"Do you read Welsh fluently?"

"No, sir, I can only read a little but I am doing my very best to learn."

"Were you at school before beginning to teach?" asked Mr Charles, more and more interested in the young man who stood so meekly before him.

"No, sir. I never had a day's schooling in my life."

"And did your parents not teach you to read while you were at home?"

"No, sir, my parents could not read a word for themselves."

Mr Charles opened his Bible at the first chapter of the Epistle to the Hebrews and asked Lewis Williams to read the opening verses.

Slowly, hesitatingly and with several mistakes the young man did as he was asked, stumbling with difficulty through the first verse.

"That will do, my lad," said Mr Charles, "but how you are able to teach others to read passes my comprehension. Tell me now how you instruct the children."

Then the poor young teacher described the methods which he had used for receiving and giving instruction. He gave an account of his musical A B C, the lessons given to himself by Betty Evans, the readings and discussions with the grammar-school boys and the students playing at "little soldiers".

As Lewis Williams proceeded with his confessions (for that was how they appeared to him), Mr Charles, with the discernment which seems to have been one of his characteristics, had seen through the roughness and awkwardness of the speaker to the real force of character and earnestness of the man. He saw that this humble follower of the Saviour had earnestly endeavoured to improve his own talent and work with it in the Master's service and that he only needed help in the development of his ability to make him a most valuable servant of Christ. He therefore recommended that Williams should place himself under the tuition of John Jones for a while so that he could be trained for efficient teaching.

During the following three months,

Lewis Williams followed the advice of Mr Charles and this was all the schooling that he ever had.

His self-development did not, however, cease with the help gained from John Jones. Every hour he could spare was devoted to study in order to prepare himself for one of the schoolmasters' places under Mr Charles's special control and management. And we are told that in order to perfect himself further in reading he used to visit neighbouring churches to study the delivery and reading of the ministers who preached there. His earnest desire was fulfilled at last, for in the year 1799 - that is, when he was about twenty-five years of age - he was engaged by Mr Charles as a paid teacher in one of his schools. He was then moved to Abergynolwyn a year later, and here, among his pupils, was our young friend Mary Jones.

In his subsequent years of work he brought about the establishing of many new schools and the reviving of others which were losing their vitality. Eventually he even became a preacher, so great was his zeal in his Master's service and so anxious was he that everyone should know the truth and join in the work of the Lord.

He died in his eighty-eighth year and was remembered with sincere gratitude and deep love by the many whom he had benefited.

Our story now returns to Mary Jones, who, at the time that Lewis Williams became schoolmaster at Abergynolwyn, was nearly sixteen years old.

She was an active, healthy girl, full of life and energy and as earnest and as diligent as ever. Nor had her purpose faltered for one moment as regarded the purchase of a Bible.

Through six long years she had hoarded every penny, denying herself the little indulgences which the poverty of her life must have made doubly attractive to someone so young. She had continued her visits to the farm-house and, while she studied her Bible lessons for school there, her desire to possess

God's Holy Book for herself grew almost to a passion.

What joy it would be, she often thought, if every day she could read and commit to memory portions of Scripture, storing her mind and heart with immortal truths. "But the time will come," she had added, "when I shall have my Bible. Yes, even though I have waited so long, the time will come." Then on her knees beside her little bed she had prayed aloud, "Dear Lord, let the time come quickly!"

As you can imagine, Mary was the great pride and delight of her parents. She was more useful and more her mother's right hand than ever and her father, as he looked into her clear, honest, intelligent dark eyes and heard her recite her lesson for school or recount for his benefit all the explanations that she had listened to that day, thanked the Lord in his heart for his brave, God-fearing child and prayed that she might grow up to be a blessing to all with whom she might have to do in the future.

On the Way

A strong, brave heart, and a purpose true,
Are better than wealth untold,
Planting a garden in barren ways,
And turning their dust to gold.

"O mother! O father! Just think! Mrs Evans has paid me for that work I did for her and it is more than I expected. Now I find I have enough to buy a Bible. I'm so happy I don't know what to do."

Mary had just come from the farm-house and now, as she bounded in with the joyful news, Jacob stopped his loom and held out both hands.

"Is it really so, Mary? After six years saving! Now then, God be thanked, child, who first put the wish into your heart and then gave you patience to wait and work to get the thing you wanted. Bless you, my little maid," and Jacob laid a hand solemnly upon his daughter's head, adding in a lower tone, "and she shall be blest!"

"But tell me, father dear," said Mary, after a little pause, "where am I to buy the Bible? There are no Bibles to be had here or at Abergynolwyn."

"I cannot tell you, Mary, but our preacher William Huw will know," replied Jacob. "You should go to him tomorrow, and ask him how you're to get the book,"

Acting upon her father's suggestion, Mary went the next day to Llechwedd to William Huw and to him she put the question so all-important to her. But he replied that no copy could be obtained (even of the Welsh version published the year before) any nearer than from Mr Charles of Bala and he added that he would be afraid that all the Bibles received by Mr Charles from London had been sold or promised to people months ago.

This was discouraging news and Mary went home, cast down indeed, but not in despair. There was still, she reflected, a chance that one copy of the Scriptures still remained in Mr Charles's possession and if so, that Bible would be hers.

The long distance of over twenty-five miles, the unknown road, the well-known, but to her, strange minister, who was to grant her the gift she longed for - all this, even if it frightened her a little, did not for one moment threaten to change her purpose.

Even Jacob and Molly, who at first, because of the distance, objected to her walking to Bala for the purchase of her Bible, ceased objecting to her wishes, "For," said good Jacob to his wife, "if it's the Lord answering our prayers and leading the child, as we prayed He might, it would wrong for us to go against His wisdom."

And so our little Mary had her way. Having received permission for her journey, she went to a neighbour living near, and telling her of her proposed expedition, asked if she would lend her a bag to carry home the treasured Bible, should she obtain it.

The neighbour, remembering Mary's many little acts of kindness towards herself and her children and glad of any way in which she could show her grateful feelings and sympathy, put the leather bag into the girl's hand and wished her good-bye with a hearty "God's speed to you!"

The next morning, a fresh, breezy day in spring in the year 1800, Mary rose almost as soon as it was light and washed and dressed with special care, for this was going to be a day of days - the day for which she had waited for years and which must, she thought, make her the happiest of girls or bring to her more grief and disappointment than she had ever known.

Her one pair of shoes - far too precious a possession to be worn on a twenty-five mile walk - Mary placed in her bag, intending to put them on as soon as she reached the town.

Although it was early, Molly and Jacob were both up to give Mary her breakfast of hot milk and bread and have family prayer, offering a special petition for God's blessing on their child and for His protection and care during her journey.

This strengthened and comforted Mary and, kissing her parents, she went out into the dawn of that lovely day - a day which lived in her memory till the last hour of her long and useful life.

She set off at a good pace - not too quick for that would have wearied her before a quarter of her journey could be accomplished, but an even steady walk, her bare brown feet treading lightly but firmly along the road, her head erect, her clear eyes glistening, her cheeks with a healthy flush under the brown skin. So she went - the bonniest, most cheerful girl in all the surrounding countryside on that sweet spring morning. Never before had everything about her looked to Mary as it looked on that memorable morning. The dear old mountain seemed to gaze down protectingly upon her. The very sun, as it came upon the eastern horizon, appeared to have a smile specially for her. The larks soared from the meadow till their trilling died away in the sky like a tuneful prayer sent up to God. The rabbits peeped out at her from leafy nooks and holes and even a squirrel, as it ran up a tree, stopped to glance familiarly at our little maiden. And the girl's heart was attuned to the joyful loveliness of nature, full of thankfulness for the past and hope for the future.

And now, leaving our heroine bravely winding her way towards Bala,

we will just record briefly the history of that good and earnest man on whom the child's hopes and expectations were this day fixed and who therefore, in Mary's eyes, must be the greatest and most important person - for the time - in the world.

But apart from the ideas and opinions of a simple girl, Thomas Charles of Bala was in reality a person of great influence and high standing in Wales. He had been instrumental in the organization and execution of much important and excellent work in places where ignorance and darkness had had the upper hand. So he came to be known by the name of "the Apostolic Charles of Bala".

He was now about fifty years of age and had spent twenty years in going about through the wildest parts of Wales, preaching the Word of Life, forming schools and using his great and varied talents in the service of his Master.

At the age of eighteen he had given himself to the Saviour, and his first work for the Lord was in his own home where he introduced family worship and exerted an influence for good, as powerful as it was loving and gentle.

His education was begun at Carmarthen and continued at Oxford, and we learn that the Rev. John Newton was a kind and good friend to him during a part of his student life and that on one occasion his vacation was spent at the house of this excellent man.

The Rev. Thomas Charles became an ordained minister of the Church of England in due course but, owing to the faithful and outspoken style of his preaching, many of his own denomination took offence and would not receive him, so he left the Church of England and joined the Welsh Calvinistic Methodists. His greatest work had been the establishment of Day and Sunday Schools in Wales. The organization of these, the selection of paid teachers, the periodical visiting and examination of the various schools, made Mr Charles's life a very busy one. But as he toiled on he could see that his labour was not in vain. Wherever he went, carrying the good news, proving it in his life, spending all he was and all he had in the service of Christ, the darkness that hung over the people lifted and the true light began to shine.

The ignorance and immorality gave place to a desire for knowledge and holiness and the soil that was barren and stony became the planting-place of sweet flowers and pleasant fruits.

Such, in brief, was the man - and that had been his work up to the time of Mary Jones's journey to Bala.

About the middle of the day Mary stopped to rest and to eat some food which her mother had provided for her. Under a tree in a grassy hollow not far from the road, she half reclined, protected from the sun by the tender green of the spring foliage and cooling her hot dusty feet in the soft damp grass that spread like a velvet carpet all over the hollow.

Before long she spied a little stream trickling down a hill on its way to the sea and here she drank and washed her face, hands and feet and was refreshed.

Half an hour's quiet, in the shade of the tree, rested her thoroughly. Then she jumped up, slung her bag over her shoulder again and recommenced her journey.

The rest of the way, along a dusty road for most of the time, and under a warm sun, was fatiguing enough but the young girl plodded patiently on though her feet were blistered and cut with stones, her head ached and her limbs were very weary.

Once a kind woman, as she passed, gave her a drink of butter-milk and a farmer's little daughter, as Mary neared her destination, offered her a share of the supper she was eating as she sat in the porch in the cool of the evening, but these were all the adventures or incidents in Mary's journey till she got to Bala.

On arriving there, she followed the instructions that had been given her by William Huw and went to the house of David Edwards, a much respected Methodist preacher at Bala.

This good man received her most kindly, questioned her as to her motive in coming so far but ended by telling her that owing to Mr Charles's early and regular routine (one secret of the large amount of work which he accomplished) it was now too late in the day to see him.

"But," added the kind old man, seeing his young visitor's disappointment, "you shall sleep here tonight and we will go to Mr Charles's as soon as I see light in his study-window tomorrow morning so that you may accomplish your errand in good time and be able to reach home before night falls."

With grateful thanks, Mary accepted the hospitality offered to her and after a simple supper she was shown into the little boxroom where she was to sleep.

There, after repeating a chapter of the Bible and offering an earnest prayer, she lay down, her mind and body both resting, her faith sure that her journey would not be in vain, but that He who had led her safely this far would give her her heart's desire.

And the curtains of night fell softly about the good preacher's humble dwelling, shadowing the sleepers there. The rest of those sleepers was sweet and their safety assured, for watching over them was the God of the night and day - the God whom they loved and trusted and underneath them were the Everlasting Arms.

Tears that Prevail

Often the tears of joy and sorrow meet;
Marah's bitter waters turn'd to sweet.

Bala is a little town, situated near the end of Bala Lake, on the north side of a wide cultivated valley. At the time of this story it was even more quiet and rural. The scenery was pastoral, hilly rather than mountainous, but well wooded and watered. The town was a favourite resort of people fond of shooting and fishing. Altogether it was a pretty, cheerful, healthy spot although lacking the imposing grandeur and rugged beauty of many other parts of North Wales.

Such, then, was the place to which our little heroine's weary feet had brought her the previous evening and such was the home - for the greater part of his life - of Thomas Charles of Bala.

Mary's deep, dreamless sleep was not broken until her host knocked at her door at early dawning.

"Wake up, Mary Jones, my child! Mr Charles is an early riser and will soon be at work. The dawn is breaking; get up, dear!"

Mary jumped up, rubbing her eyes. The time had really come, then, and in a few minutes she would know what was to be the result of her long waiting.

Her heart beat quicker as she washed and dressed but her excitement calmed when she sat down for a minute or two on the side of her bed and repeated the 23rd Psalm.

The sweet words of the royal singer were the first that occurred to her, and now, as she murmured, "The Lord is my shepherd, I shall not want," she felt as though she was truly being watched over and cared for by a loving Shepherd and being led by Him.

She was soon ready and David Edwards and his guest proceeded together to Mr Charles's house.

"There's a light in his study," said the good old preacher. "Our apostle is at his desk already. There are not many like him, Mary; always at work for the Master. The world would be better if we had more men like him."

Mary did not reply, but she listened intently as David Edwards knocked at the door. There was no answer, only the tread of footsteps across the floor above and the next moment the door opened and Mr Charles himself stood before them.

"Good morning, friend Edwards! And what brings you here so early? Come in, do," said the friendly hearty voice, which so many knew and had reason to love. Then, as David Edwards entered, Mr Charles noticed the little figure behind him in the doorway.

A rather timid, shrinking little figure it was now, for Mary's courage was fast ebbing away and she felt shy and frightened. A few words of explanation passed between the old preacher and Mr Charles then Mary was invited to enter the study.

"Now, my child," said Mr Charles, "don't be afraid but tell me about yourself, where you live, what your name is and what you want."

At this Mary took courage and answered all Mr Charles's questions, her voice (which at first was low and tremulous) strengthening as her courage returned. She told him all about her home and her parents, her longing when she was only a child for a Bible of her own, then of the long years during which she had saved up her little earnings towards the purchase of a Bible - the sum being now complete.

Then Mr Charles examined her as to her Scripture knowledge and was delighted with the little girl's intelligent replies, which showed how earnestly and thoroughly she had studied the Book she loved so well.

"But how, my child," said he, "did you get to know the Bible as you do when you did not own one?"

Then Mary told him of the visits to the farm-house and how, through the kindness of the farmer and his wife, she had been able to study her

Sunday-school lessons and commit portions of Scripture to memory.

As she informed Mr Charles of all that had taken place and he began to realize how brave, patient, earnest and hopeful she had been through all these years of waiting and how far she had now come to obtain possession of the coveted treasure, his bright face became over-shadowed, and turning to David Edwards, he said, sadly, "I am indeed sorry that this dear girl should have come all the way from Llanfihangel to buy a Bible and that I should be unable to supply her with one. The consignment of Welsh Bibles that I received from London last year was all sold out months ago, except for a few copies which I have kept for friends whom I must not disappoint. Unfortunately, the Society which has supplied Wales with the Scriptures until now declines to print any more and I do not know where to get Welsh Bibles to satisfy our country's need."

Until now, Mary had been looking up into Mr Charles's face with her great dark eyes full of hope and confidence but as he spoke these words to David Edwards and she noticed his overclouded face and began to understand the full impact of his words, the room seemed to her to darken suddenly, and, dropping into the nearest seat, she buried her face in her hands and sobbed as, perhaps, few girls of her age had ever sobbed before.

It was all over, then, she said to herself - all of no use - the prayers, the longing, the waiting, the working, the saving for six long years, the weary tramp with bare feet, the near prospect of her hopes being fulfilled, all, all in vain! And to a mind so stocked with Bible texts as hers, the language of the Psalmist seemed the natural outburst for so great a grief, "Hath God forgotten to be gracious? Hath He in anger shut up His tender mercies?" All in vain

- all of no use! And the poor little head, recently so erect, drooped lower and lower and the sunburnt hands, roughened with work and exposure, could not hide the great hot tears that rolled down, chasing each other over cheeks out of which the usual rosy tint had gone, and falling unheeded through her fingers.

There were a few moments during which only Mary's sobs broke the silence but those sobs had appealed to Mr Charles's heart with a feeling of pity which he was unable to resist.

With his own voice broken and unsteady, he said, as he rose from his seat, and laid a hand on the drooping head of the girl before him: "My dear child, I see you *must* have a Bible, difficult as it is for me to spare you one. It is impossible, yes, simply impossible, to refuse you."

In the sudden reversal of feeling that followed these words, Mary could not speak. She glanced up with such

a face of mingled rain and sunshine
- such a rainbow smile - such a look of
inexpressible joy and thankfulness in
her brimming eyes that the responsive
tears gushed to the eyes of both Mr
Charles and David Edwards.

Mr Charles turned away for a
moment to a book-cupboard that stood
behind him, and opening it, he drew
out a Bible.

Then, laying a hand once more on
Mary's head, with the other he placed

the Bible in her grasp and looking down into the earnest, glistening eyes upturned to him, he said, "If you, my dear girl, are glad to receive this Bible, truly glad am I to be able to give it to you. Read it carefully, study it diligently, treasure up the sacred words in your memory and act upon its teachings."

And then, as Mary, quite overcome with delight and thankfulness, began once more to sob, but softly and with sweet, happy tears, Mr Charles turned to the old preacher and said huskily, "David Edwards, is not such a sight as this enough to melt the hardest heart? A girl, so young, so poor, so intelligent, so familiar with Scripture, compelled to walk all the distance from Llanfihangel to Bala (about fifty miles there and back) to get a Bible! From this day on I can never rest until I find some way of supplying the real need of my country that cries out for the Word of God."

Half an hour later, Mary Jones, having shared David Edwards's frugal breakfast, set off on her homeward journey.

The day was somewhat cloudy but the child did not notice it as her heart was full of sunshine. The wind blew strongly but a great calm was in her soul and her young face was so full of happiness that the folk she met on the way could not but notice her as she tripped joyfully on, her bare feet seeming hardly to press the ground, her eyes shining with deep content, while the bag containing her newly-found treasure was no longer slung across her back, but clasped close to her chest.

The sun rose and burst through the clouds, glorifying all the landscape and onward steadily went Mary, her heart, like the lark's song, full of thanksgiving and her voice breaking out now and again into melody, to which the words of some old hymn or of a well-known and much-loved text set themselves, without an effort on the girl's part.

On, still on, she went, not noticing the length and weariness of the way.

The afternoon came and the sun set in the western heavens with a glory that made Mary think of the home prepared above for God's children; that heaven with its walls of jasper, its gates of pearl, its streets of gold and its light that needs nor sun nor moon but streams from the Life-giving Presence of God Himself

That evening Jacob and his wife were seated waiting for supper and for Mary. What news would the child bring? How had she got on? Had she received her Bible? These were some of the questions which the anxious parents asked themselves, listening all the while for their daughter's return after the weariness and possible dangers of her fifty-mile walk.

But the worthy couple were not kept long in suspense.

Soon the light step which they knew so well approached the cottage. The latch was lifted and Mary entered, weary, foot-sore, dusty and travel-stained indeed but with happiness dimpling her cheeks and flashing in her eyes. And Jacob held out both arms to his darling and as he clasped her to his heart he murmured, in the words of the prophet of old, "Is it well with the child?" and Mary, from the depths of a satisfied heart, answered solemnly but with gladness, "It is well."

We sometimes see - and particularly in the case of young people - that great eagerness for the possession of some coveted article can be followed by indifference and lack of interest when the treasure is safely in their hands. It was not so, however, with Mary Jones. The Bible for which she had toiled, waited, prayed and wept became each day more precious to her. The Word of the Lord was indeed near to her, even in her mouth and in her heart.

Chapter after chapter was learned by heart and the study of the Sunday-school lessons became her greatest privilege and delight.

If a question were asked by the teacher, which other girls could not answer, Mary was always turned to and was invariably ready with a thoughtful, intelligent reply and in committing to memory not only chapters, but whole books of the Bible, she was unrivalled both in the school and neighbourhood.

This wasn't all. For though to love, read and learn the Bible are good things, this is not the sum of what is required by Him who has said: "If ye love Me, *keep* My commandments."

Mary's study of the Word of God did not prevent the more than ever faithful carrying out of all her duties. Her mother, who had at one time feared that Mary's desire for book learning and longing to possess a Bible of her own might lead her to the neglect of her practical duties, was surprised and delighted to see that although there was a change indeed in the girl, it was a change for the better.

The holy truths that sank into her heart were but the precious seed in good ground, which brings forth fruit an hundredfold and the more entire the setting apart of that young heart to the Lord, the sweeter became even the most routine duties of life because they were done for Him.

Not very long after Mary's visit to Bala, she had the great pleasure of seeing again her kind friend with whom, in her memory, her beloved Bible would now always be associated.

Mr Charles, in the course of his periodical visits to the various villages where his circulating schools were established, came to Abergynolwyn to inspect the school there under the charge of Lewis Williams and by examining the children personally to assure himself of their progress.

Among the bright young faces upturned to him his observant eye soon caught sight of one face that he had cause to remember with special and with deep interest. The interest deepened still more, when he found that from her alone all his most difficult questions received replies and that her intelligence was only surpassed by the childlike humility which is one mark of the true Christian.

We may be very sure that Mr Charles did not miss this opportunity of saying a few kind words to his young friend and that Mary in her turn treasured them up and remembered them through the many years and the various events of her later life.

The Work Begun

Henceforward, the olive-leaf plucked off,
Carried to every nation,
Shall promise be of re-awakening life,
Our sinful world's salvation.

We have seen that the incident recorded in the last chapter made a deep impression on the mind and heart of Mr Charles. The thought of that bare-footed child, her weary journey, her eagerness to spend her six year's savings in the purchase of a Bible, her bitter tears of disappointment and her sweet tears of joy - all these came back to his recollection again and again, blended with the memory of ignorance and darkness of too many of his countrymen and with the cry that was coming from all over Wales for the Word of God.

The girl's story was only an illustration of the terrible sense of spiritual death that had the upper hand during this famine of Bibles. No-one could know so well as this good man - whose influence was, from the nature of his work, very widely spread - how deep a need lay at the root of the people's lack of devotion to God, against which he seemed, with all his earnest striving, to be making such slow progress. It is no surprise, then, that the question of how to secure the publication of enough copies of God's Word for Wales continually occupied his mind.

In the winter of 1802 Mr Charles visited London, full of this one great thought and purpose, though not as yet seeing how it was to be accomplished.

It was while turning the matter over in his mind one morning that the idea occurred to him of a society for the spreading of the Scriptures, a society whose only objective would be the publication and distribution of God's Holy Word.

Consulting with some of his friends who belonged to the Committee of the Religious Tract Society, Mr Charles received the warmest sympathy and encouragement. He was then introduced at their next meeting where he spoke powerfully and with feeling about Wales and its need for Bibles. He illustrated this need by telling the story which forms the subject of our little book and this really brought home his appeal on behalf of the people of Wales.

His appeal had impact. A wave of sympathy for a people that so longed and thirsted for the Word of God ran through the meeting.

An earnest desire took hold of Mr Charles's hearers and urged them to do something towards supplying this great need.

The hearts of many were further stirred, and their sympathies aroused, when one of the secretaries of the Committee, the Reverend Joseph Hughes, rose and in reply to Mr Charles's appeal for Bibles for Wales, exclaimed enthusiastically: "Mr Charles, surely a society can be formed to meet the need for Bibles; and if it can be done for Wales, why not for the world?"

This Christian tender-heartedness found an echo in the hearts of many among the audience, and the secretary was instructed to prepare a letter inviting Christians everywhere, and of all denominations, to unite in forming a society which would have the objective of spreading God's Word over the whole world.

Two years were spent in publicising the purpose of the Committee and in the administration involved in setting it up, but in March 1804, the British and Foreign Bible Society was actually established and at its first meeting contributions of £700 were received.

Unfortunately, Mr Charles was unable to be present at this meeting. He was hard at work at home in Wales, but he heard the news with the greatest joy and it was owing to his exertions and to those of his friends, as well as to the efforts of other Christian workers who deeply felt the great need of the people at this time, that the contributions in

Wales amounted to nearly £1,900, most of this consisting of the subscriptions and donations of the lower and poorer classes.

In the foundation of the Bible Society all denominations met and were brought thus into sympathy by a common cause and an earnest wish to serve one common Master. Hence we see representatives of all Christian Churches working together for the good and enlightenment of the world.

Meanwhile, wherever Mr Charles was at work, wherever his influence extended there was awakened the longings, and thence arose the petition for the Word of Life. Wherever he told the story, either on Welsh or English platforms, of the little maiden of Llanfihangel, the simple narrative never failed to carry home some lessons to the heart of each hearer.

Great was the joy and thankfulness of this single-minded and hard-working minister of Christ, when he learned that the first resolution of the Committee of the Bible Society was to bring out an edition of the Welsh Bible for the use of Welsh Sunday schools. His delight was greater still when the first consignment of these Bibles reached Bala in 1806.

Among the most useful workers in the early years of the Bible Society was the Reverend John Owen who soon became one of its secretaries and proved to be a most earnest and able promoter of the glorious enterprise.

Associated also with this time of the great Society's childhood are the honoured names of Steinkopff, Wilberforce and Josiah Pratt. While in Wales, among its earliest supporters, were Dr. Warren, Bishop of Bangor, who united cordially with Mr Charles and others in the good work. As to Mr Charles, he displayed the deepest interest in this new work in many practical ways up to the time of his death.

But in following the work of the Bible Society we must not forget our friend Mary Jones who during this time had passed from early girlhood to womanhood.

On leaving school she worked as a weaver and we conclude that she was still living with her parents.

Of one thing we may be sure; that her precious Bible was as dear to her as ever and that she was intensely interested in the setting up of the Bible

Society and in the news of the first edition of Welsh Bibles having been received at Bala.

But in addition to her weaving and the household help she gave her mother, who was not so well or strong as before, Mary had developed a talent for dressmaking, which stood her in good stead when she needed to earn a little extra money.

Anyone who could afford it came to her to cut out and make their dresses and though Mary never wasted a moment she sometimes found it quite difficult to fit in everything in the day that she planned to do.

As for Jacob, his asthma became more and more of a problem and when the winter winds and fogs came he suffered a lot, although he was always brave and patient, "for the dear Lord's sake," who had borne so much for him.

Occasionally, Mr Charles would visit Abergynolwyn and every now and then Llanfihangel and then he and Mary Jones met again and she would learn from him how the Society in London was going on - the great London which was a strange, distant and unknown world to her. She only had vague ideas of its size and its distance from the little, quiet, secluded place where she lived.

And so, up in London, the great tree of life went on spreading, and growing, from a root which had sprung in Wales.

Youthful Promise Fulfilled

Nurtured of Heaven, the blossom bloom'd
Until an open flower,
With buds around it, gazed upon the sun,
Or drank the shower;
Nor did forget, in this the blooming time,
The fragrance due
To Him who gives to Nature all her wealth,
To flowers their hue.

When we meet our heroine of Llanfihangel again, she is no longer Mary Jones. A great change has come to her life and her school work and old home life with her parents are things of the past. For she has married a weaver, called Thomas Lewis, and is living at the village of Bryncrug, near Towyn, not very far from Llanfihangel. But the difference in circumstances has not changed the character of Mary.

So dutiful and devoted a daughter as Mary had ever proved herself would hardly have left her parents while she could care for them in their declining years, work for them, and be their great joy and comfort.

So it is only reasonable to suppose that before she married both good old Jacob and his wife had been laid to rest and that Mary, in casting in her lot with Thomas Lewis whom possibly she had known for many years, would be neglecting no duty that could be required from a loving daughter.

But here, at Bryncrug, with a husband and children of her own and the care of a home for which she alone was responsible, with new duties and fresh cares, Mary's love for her Bible had grown, not diminished.

Other things had changed -companionships, home influences, responsibilities, interests - but the Sacred Word remained the same, except that every day it grew more into her heart and became more and more part of her life. In answer to careful study and sincere prayers for God's Spirit to give her insight, Mary's Bible brought her an understanding of deep meanings of truth and sweetness which she had not known before.

If Mary's life was a busy one during the years spent at Llanfihangel, her life was twice as busy here at Bryncrug. But the same quiet energy and dedication which had always made her remarkable still influenced everything that she did, making every duty, however insignificant and everyday, a service for Christ. Meanwhile, by her consistent Christian walk and example she influenced for good everyone she met.

If a neighbour's child wanted to have a Sunday-school lesson explained they invariably came to Mary, who could always spare a few minutes to pass on the teaching that had been so precious to her in her childhood. And her intimate knowledge of the Bible gave her a very clear way of explaining its truths, while her insight into character and her sympathetic nature made her a wise counsellor and an excellent teacher.

If a friend wanted a hint or two about making a new dress or advice on the management of her bee-hives, Mary was always the authority appealed to as she was the most capable and the kindest of neighbours and always ready to lend a helping hand, or speak a helpful word.

So, in Bryncrug she was winning for herself the love and confidence of the people of her new home village and showing in life and character the glory of that Saviour whose faithful servant she tried to be.

We have just mentioned that she was considered an authority in the management of bees and so she should have been, as her success with her own bee-hives sufficiently proved.

That success was simply remarkable, both as to the large number of hives and their profitable results.

The attracting power and influence which Mary seemed to exercise over people appeared to extend even to her bees because we are told that whenever she approached the hives, her reception by her winged friends was nothing less than royal, such was the loyalty and enthusiasm of these sensible, busy little honey-makers.

The air would be thick with buzzing swarms and in time they would settle on her by hundreds, covering her from head to foot, walking over her, but never attempting to sting or show any feeling but one of absolute confidence and friendliness. She would even catch a handful of them as though they were flies - but softly, so as not to hurt them - and they never misunderstood her or gave her the slightest injury. In short, there seemed to be a sort of unspoken agreement between Mary and her bees and what was earned by their work was used to support of God's work in the world. For Mary divided the proceeds as follows.

The money brought by the sale of the honey was used for the family and household expenses but the proceeds of the wax were divided among the societies which, poor as she was, Mary was delighted to assist.

Among these, first in her estimation stood the British and Foreign Bible Society, whose establishment she had been so closely connected with, and she was never happier than when she could spare what for her was a large amount to help in sending the Word of God - so precious to her own heart - all over the world.

Mary was also much interested in the Calvinistic Methodist Missionary Society - the Society founded by the denomination to which she had, for so many years, belonged.

Mary was sitting at her cottage

door one day when a neighbour, Betsy Davies, came up. "Good day, Mary," said she; "may I come and sit with you for an hour this afternoon? I've a dress I must alter for my eldest girl and I don't see how to begin, so I thought maybe you'd be good enough to show me."

"Yes, I'll do that with pleasure," replied Mary. "My children are all at school and my husband has gone to Towyn so I have a quiet hour or two before me. Let me see your work, Betsy."

Betsy Davies laid the garment over Mary's knee and Mary's eyes, quick and intelligent as ever, saw in a moment or two what was needed.

"That's not a difficult job," she said pleasantly, "or even a long one. Just unpick that seam, Betsy, and I'll pin it for you as it ought to be; then if you let down the tuck in the skirt, you'll have it long enough and as for the tear, I think I've got some thread about the right colour with which you can darn it up. I will show you, my dear, how I darn my little Mary's dresses when she tears them, as she does very often, playing with her brothers. Yours can be mended in just the same way and you'll find that the repair will hardly show at all."

When the two women settled down to their work, Betsy said "I wish you'd

tell me, Mary, how you manage to get on as you do. You can't be rich people, your husband being only a weaver like mine and like most of the others here and yet you never get into debt and you always seem to have enough for yourselves. What's more wonderful still is that you've enough to give away something too. I must say, I can't understand it!"

"I don't think there's anything very hard to understand," said Mary, smiling. "If by great care and a little self-denial we can contribute something to help in God's work, it is surely the greatest joy we can have."

"Yes, that's all very well," replied Betsy, "but I never have anything to contribute and I haven't as many children as you, so my family and housekeeping won't cost so much as yours."

"It's like this, Betsy dear," said Mary, "we ask ourselves - I mean my husband, my children and I, all of us

- 'What can we do without?' And each of us is willing to give up some little indulgence and so we save the money. This we put into a box which we call the treasury and whenever we add anything to what we keep there, we think of the widow who cast her two mites into the treasury of the temple, and of our Lord's kind, tender words about her."

"But what sort of things can you give up?" asked Betsy. "We poor folk, it seems to me, don't have any more than just the bare necessities of life and you can't give up eating and drinking or go without clothes on your back."

"Yet I think if you give it some thought you'll see that there are some things which are not really needful, although they may be pleasant," replied Mary. "Now, for instance Thomas had always been used to a pipe and a bit of tobacco in an evening after his work was done but when we were all wondering what we could give up for our dear Lord's sake, he said 'Well, I'll give up my smoke in the evenings.' And I tell you, Betsy, the tears came into my eyes when I heard that, knowing my husband's words meant a real sacrifice. Then our eldest son, wishing to imitate his father, cried out, 'And I've still got that Christmas box my master gave me last winter and I'll give that.' And Sally, she gave up the thought of a new hat ribbon I'd promised her and she sponged and ironed her old one instead and wore it, feeling prouder than if it had been new. And as for little Benny, he spent a whole day picking up sticks in the wood to earn a penny and that was his gift."

"And you yourself?" asked Betsy, with interest.

"Me? Oh, I have the wax that my bees make and the money that I got by selling that went into the treasury, as well as any other small amount I did not actually need. And this I must say,

Betsy, we have never really suffered by giving anything to God and He repays us with the happiness and contentment that He alone can give."

"That I can well believe," replied Betsy, "for I never hear you grumble, or see you look cross or discontented like the rest of the neighbours and as I do myself only too often. Well, Mary," she continued, "I intend to try your plan, though it will be very hard at first as I'm not used to that sort of saving."

"I think I got used to it when I was a child, putting away my little mites of money towards buying a Bible," rejoined Mary. "For six years I put aside all my little earnings and since then it has become natural to me."

"You did get your Bible, then?"

"Yes, indeed; this is the very one," and rising from her seat Mary took the much prized volume from the little table in the cottage and put in into her visitor's hands.

Betsy looked at it, inside and out and then handed it back, saying, "I really believe, Mary, that this Bible is one of the reasons why you are so different from all the rest of us. You've read and studied and learned so much of it that your thoughts and words and life are full of it."

And Mary turned her bright dark eyes, now full of happy tears, to her companion and answered, in a broken voice, "Oh, Betsy dear, if there is even a little truth in which you kindly say of me, I thank God that in His great mercy and love He allows me, poor and weak and simple as I am, to show in my small way His glory and the truth of His blessed Word."

Her Works Do Follow Her

O mighty tree, o'ershadowing all the earth,
In loneliest wilds thy seedling had its birth.

Now our story nears its close. The last glimpse of our friend Mary shows us an aged woman in the curious traditional Welsh dress.

She holds in one hand a staff for the support of her trembling limbs, once so active and nimble while with the other she clasps to her side her beloved Bible, the companion of so many years, the consoler and comforter, the guide and teacher of her life.

How much of joy or of sorrow, of trial or of what the world calls success, had fallen to Mary's lot during her long life of eighty-two years, we do not know but we do learn that she had eight children, several of whom may have died in early life.

We know little of Mary's actual experiences but it was impossible that during her married life she would not have learned what deep sorrow meant as it is almost certain that she survived several of her children and that her husband also died before she did.

Still, since we are taught that God's children do not sorrow as those without hope, so we are sure that the childlike, trusting spirit of this handmaid of the Lord was as ready to suffer as to do the will of her Divine Master.

Our once bright, bonny and blithe maiden was now feeble and tottering but it was only physically that Mary had altered. She was still the same brave, simple-hearted, earnest and faithful follower of Christ. Time with its changes, in parting her from most of those whom she loved on earth, had not separated her from the love of Jesus or taken away her delight in the Word of the Lord that endureth for ever.

Indeed she loved her Bible more than ever because she understood it more fully and had proved its truth beyond all doubting, again and again, in her daily life for so many years.

No doubt, then, when the summons came and she heard the voice which she had known and loved from childhood, saying to her, 'Come up higher!" she wasn't afraid but felt that surely since goodness and mercy had followed her all the days of her life she should dwell in the house of the Lord - that house above, not made with hands - for ever.

Mary Jones died on December the 28th, 1866, at the good old age of eighty-two. We have no information about her last moments, except that on her deathbed she bequeathed her precious Bible to the Rev. Robert Griffiths, who in his turn bequeathed it to Mr Rees.

This Bible, which is now in the possession of the British and Foreign Bible Society, is a thick volume of the edition published by the Society for the Promotion of Christian Knowledge in 1799 - the last edition of the Welsh Bible before the establishment of the Bible Society. It also contains, in Mary Jones's handwriting - in perhaps the first English that she had learned - a note that she bought it in the year 1800, when she was sixteen years old.

So, full of days, and like Dorcas in the New Testament, of good works, Mary Jones passed away from earth to the rest that remains for the people of God; a sheaf of ripe corn safely gathered at last into the heavenly granary.

She was buried in the little churchyard at Bryncrug and a stone was raised to her memory by those who loved to recall the influence of her beautiful life and the important, if humble, part she had taken in the founding of the great work of the British and Foreign Bible Society.

So from small beginnings great things grew and during the first three years following the establishment of the Society, it circulated almost 82,000 Bibles and Testaments.

When the Society was founded the Bible existed in less than fifty languages. Since then, the Society has continued to do all it can to make God's word available across the world through its support for translation work.

Today, the Bible Society also brings the power and influence of the Bible to people through the media, curriculum resources for schools, training seminars, biblical storytelling workshops, tape ministries, worldwide Bible distribution programmes and other projects.

To find out more about the work of
the British and Foreign Bible Society,
you should contact:-

Bible Society
Stonehill Green
Westlea
Swindon
SN5 7DG

info@bfbs.org.uk
www.biblesociety.org.uk

If by reading this book, just one heart
is moved to a more earnest work for
the Master, to self-denial and loving
service in the spread of His truth, to a
more eager study of God's Word and a
greater zeal in circulating and making
it known amongst others - then indeed
this little story of a poor Welsh girl and
her Bible will not have been written in
vain.

Classic Fiction

The Basket of Flowers

By Christoph Von Schmid

Mary grows up sheltered and secure in a beautiful cottage with a loving father. She learns lessons about humility, purity and forgiveness under her father's watchful gaze. However, even though she loves God and obeys him this does not protect her from the envy and hatred of others. Mary is given a generous gift of a new dress from her rich friend Amelia. This incites envy from Juliette, Amelia's maid, who had wanted the dress for herself. When Amelia's mother's ring goes missing Juliette blames Mary. Both Mary and her father are evicted from their home. But even when Mary doubts if she will ever clear her name she turns to God who is a constant source of comfort to her. Who did steal the ring in the end? That is the final unexpected twist in the tale which makes this book a really good read.

ISBN 1-85792 -525-4

Classic Fiction

Christie's Old Organ

By O F Walton

Christie knows what it is like to be homeless and on the streets - that's why he is overjoyed to be given a roof over his head by Old Treffy, the Organ Grinder. But Treffy is old and sick and Christie is worried about him. All that Treffy wants is to have peace in his heart and a home of his own. That is what Christie wants too. Christie hears about how Heaven is like Home Sweet Home. Every time he plays it on Treffy's barrel organ he wonders if he and Treffy can find their way to God's special home. Find out how God uses Christie and the old Barrel organ and lots of friends along the way to bring Treffy and Christie to their own Home Sweet Home.

ISBN: 1-85792-523-8

Classic Fiction

A Peep Behind The Scenes

By O F Walton

Rosalie and her mother are tired of living a life with no home and precious little hope. But Rosalie's father runs a travelling theatre company and the whole family is forced to travel from one town to the next year in year out. Rosalie's mother remembers a better life, before she was married when she had parents who loved her and a sister to play with. Through her memories Rosalie is introduced to the family she never knew she had. Rosalie and her mother are also introduced to somebody else - The Good Shepherd. They hear for the first time about the God who loves them and wants to rescue them and take them to his own home in Heaven. But what does the future hold for Rosalie? Will God help her find her family as he helped her find him? Of course he will!

ISBN 1-85792 -524-6

Children's Talks

by D L Moody

D L Moody was one of the great evangelists of the 19th century and preached to millions throughout his life. When he visited London for a four-month stay the attendance at his meetings reached more than 2.5 million. But no matter how many millions listened to his every word he always retained a loving concern and prayerful interest for children. This is evident in the stories that he told. Simple stories that teach strong truths D L Moody often used examples from his own childhood or family life to explain the gospel of Jesus Christ. There are over 100 tales and anecdotes in this book making it an invaluable tool for families, teachers and church leaders.

Trailblazers

The Trailblazers series are an excellent series of books to give good role models to young people showing how Christians have been in the forefront of new ideas and adventures; travel and social justice as well as struggling against dictatorships and persecution.

John Newton:
A Slave Set Free
ISBN 1 85792 8342

Richard Wurmbrand:
A Voice in the Dark
ISBN 1 85792 2980

Robert Murray McCheyne:
Life is An Adventure
ISBN 1 85792 9470

Mary Slessor:
Servant to the Slave
ISBN 1 85792 3480

Joni Eareckson Tada;
Swimming Against the Tide
ISBN 1 85792 8334

Corrie ten Boom: The
Watchmaker's Daughter
ISBN 1 85792 116X

The Storyteller - C.S. Lewis

by Derick Bingham

C.S.Lewis loved to write stories even as a small child. He grew up to face grief when his mother died, fear when he fought in the First World War and finally love when he realised that God was a God of love and that his son Jesus Christ was the answer to his heart ache. C.S.Lewis brought this newly discovered joy and wonder into his writings and became known world-wide for his amazing Narnia stories. Read all about this fascinating man. Find out why his friends called him Jack. Find out what C.S.Lewis was really like and discover how one of the greatest writers and academics of the twentieth century turned from atheism to God.

"A good introduction to my stepfather C.S. Lewis" Douglas Gresham

ISBN 1-85792-423-1

The Watch-maker's Daughter
Corrie Ten Boom

by Jean Watson

If you like stories of adventure, courage and faith - then here's one you won't forget. Corrie loved to help others, especially handicapped children. But her happy lifestyle in Holland is shattered when she is sent to a Nazi concentration camp. She suffered hardship and punishment but experienced God's love and help in unbearable situations.

Her amazing story has been told worldwide and has inspired many people. Discover about one of the most outstanding Christian women of the 20th century.

ISBN 1-85792-116-X

Good books with the real message of hope!

Christian Focus Publications publishes biblically-accurate books for adults and children.

If you are looking for quality bible teaching for children then we have a wide and excellent range of bible story books - from board books to teenage fiction, we have it covered.

You can also try our new Bible teaching Syllabus for 3-9 year olds and teaching materials for pre-school children.

These children's books are bright, fun and full of biblical truth, an ideal way to help children discover Jesus Christ for themselves. Our aim is to help children find out about God and get them enthusiastic about reading the Bible, now and later in their lives.

**Find us at our web page:
www.christianfocus.com**